Designer Dogs

Cockapoo

A Cross between a Cocker Spaniel and a Poodle

by Sheri A. Johnson

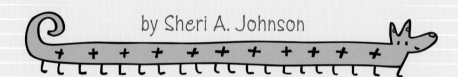

Consultant:

Tanya Dewey, PhD

University of Michigan Museum of Zoology

Ann Arbor, Michigan

CAPSTONE PRESS
a capstone imprint

Snap Books are published by Capstone Press,
1710 Roe Crest Drive, North Mankato, Minnesota 56003.
www.capstonepub.com

Books published by Capstone Press are manufactured with paper
containing at least 10 percent post-consumer waste.

Library of Congress Cataloging-in-Publication Data
Johnson, Sheri.
  Cockapoo : a cross between a Cocker Spaniel and a Poodle / by Sheri Johnson.
     p. cm.—(Snap. Designer dogs)
  Includes bibliographical references and index.
  Summary: "Describes Cockapoos, their characteristics and behavior, and includes basic information on feeding,
grooming, training, and healthcare"—Provided by publisher.
  ISBN 978-1-4296-7763-9 (library binding)
  1. Cockapoo—Juvenile literature. 1. Title.
  SF429.C54J54 2012
  636.72'8—dc23   2011036704

Editorial Credits
Editor: Lori Shores
Designer: Veronica Correia
Media Researcher: Marcie Spence
Photo Stylist: Sarah Schuette
Studio Scheduler: Marcy Morin
Production Specialist: Kathy McColley

Photo Credits:
Capstone Studio: Karon Dubke, cover (top and bottom right), 5, 6, 13, 15, 17, 18, 19, 20, 21, 23, 24, 25, 27, 28; Corbis: Ocean,
10; iStockphoto: adamkaz, 29; Shutterstock: Annette Shaff, 7, Dee Hunter, 9 (bottom), Eric Isselee, cover (bottom left), 11, Milan
Vachal, 9 (top), RTimages, 16

Printed in the United States of America in North Mankato, Minnesota.
102011   006405CGS12

Table of Contents

Chapter 1

Dogs by Design

Long hair or short? Spunky or quiet? What if you want to mix and match? How about a playful dog with a silky, low-shed coat? What **breed** is it? A Cocker Spaniel? A Poodle? Yes, it's both! It's the energetic and friendly designer dog, the Cockapoo.

A Cockapoo is a cross between a Poodle and a Cocker Spaniel. They're smart dogs that learn quickly, just like their Poodle parent. They're also known for friendliness from their Cocker Spaniel parent. These affectionate dogs form close relationships with their human families. Many people choose Cockapoos for pets. These dogs are right at home with a large family and small children. But they are equally comfortable in an apartment with one owner.

breed—a certain kind of animal within an animal group; breed also means to mate and raise a certain kind of animal

Dog Fact!

Some people call Cockapoos "cockerpoos." In Australia, they're called Spoodles!

WHAT IS A DESIGNER DOG?

Hundreds of dog breeds offer companionship to people all over the world. They generally fall into two categories. A **purebred** dog is born from two dogs of the same breed. A mutt is a mixture of several breeds or an unplanned combination of two breeds. A designer dog is a mix of two different purebred dogs. They're also called crossbreeds, although some people still call them mutts. The difference is that designer dogs are bred purposely to combine **traits** of the parent breeds.

People breed designer dogs for specific reasons. The Labradoodle was first bred to be an assistance dog for people with allergies. Cockapoos are also less likely to cause allergic reactions. Other designer dogs are bred to look a certain way or to avoid medical problems. Breeders hope crossbreeds will be less likely to suffer from health problems common in the parent breeds.

purebred—having parents of the same breed

trait—a quality or characteristic that makes one person or animal different from another

Labradoodle

Club Rules

Only purebred dogs can be registered with the American Kennel Club (AKC). The AKC does not consider designer dogs to be true breeds. To qualify as a breed, dogs must meet standards in color, size, and personality. Because designer dogs are crossbreeds, their traits are not always the same. Two Cockapoos can look and act very differently. Other dog clubs, such as the Designer Dogs Kennel Club (DDKC), provide information on mixed breeds. Breeders can register their designer dogs with these clubs.

Chapter 2

Creating a Cockapoo

Cockapoos are still new in the dog world, but their parents are not. Poodles and Cocker Spaniels are popular breeds. Some Cockapoos seem more like Cocker Spaniels. Others seem more like Poodles. To get to know the Cockapoo, you have to know the parent breeds first.

POODLES

Poodles are one of the most popular dog breeds. They are gentle and loving with a pleasant **temperament**. Poodles are also some of the smartest dogs, but that doesn't stop them from being playful. These energetic dogs need plenty of exercise daily. Poodles are people-oriented and eager to please their owners. The combination of intelligence and playfulness makes Poodles easy to train and easy to love.

temperament—the combination of an animal's behavior and personality

Choose a Size

Poodles can be one of three sizes. Standard Poodles stand more than 15 inches (38 centimeters) tall. Miniature poodles are between 11 and 15 inches (28 and 38 cm) tall. Toy poodles are much smaller at less than 10 inches (25 cm) tall. Any size Poodle can be bred with the Cocker Spaniel. The size of the poodle parent determines the size of the Cockapoo.

Poodles have thick, curly coats, but they don't all look the same. Some Poodles have soft, wavy fur. Other Poodles have coats that are coarse and wooly. Their coats don't shed, so they are good pets for people with allergies. But because they don't shed, poodles need to be brushed often to avoid tangles in their fur.

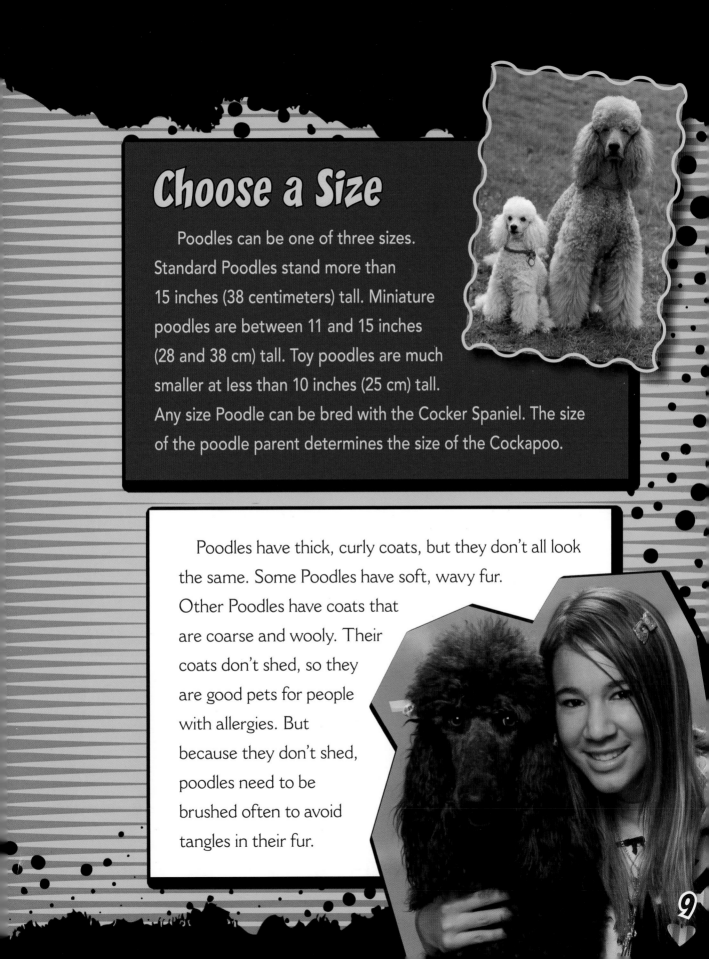

COCKER SPANIELS

Cocker Spaniels are hard-working dogs that were first used for hunting. But don't be fooled. These hunters are sweet tempered and friendly. Cocker Spaniels are popular with families. They prefer to be with people and are great with children. Like Poodles, Cocker Spaniels are eager to please their owners, which makes them easy to train. Because of these traits, Cocker Spaniels make great **therapy dogs**.

therapy dog—a dog trained to provide affection and comfort to people in need, such as sick, elderly, or disabled people

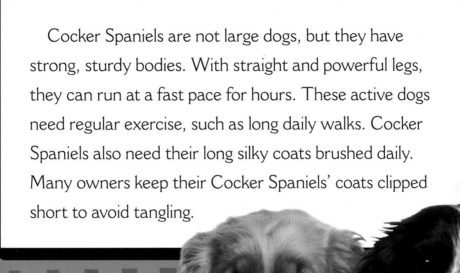

Cocker Spaniels are not large dogs, but they have strong, sturdy bodies. With straight and powerful legs, they can run at a fast pace for hours. These active dogs need regular exercise, such as long daily walks. Cocker Spaniels also need their long silky coats brushed daily. Many owners keep their Cocker Spaniels' coats clipped short to avoid tangling.

Dog Fact!

Cockapoos can also be bred from two adult Cockapoos.

Cocker Spaniels

Chapter 3

Cute and Cuddly Cockapoos

With intelligent and cheerful parents, Cockapoos are smart and sweet dogs. They are affectionate with their owners and cheerfully follow commands. Although both parents are known for hunting, Cockapoos aren't hunting dogs. These friendly dogs would rather be at home. They are usually quiet dogs, but they may bark when left alone for long periods.

Breeders can't guarantee that their Cockapoos will have all the best traits from the parent breeds. Cockapoos can have any traits of either parent. Some Cockapoos seem more like Cocker Spaniels. Others have more of a Poodle personality. But most owners say the Cockapoo is a balanced mix of the outgoing, charming Cocker Spaniel and the intelligent, people-loving Poodle.

The Cockapoo Club of America offers a description of how Cockapoos should look. The ideal Cockapoo is a quick dog with a compact body and strong legs. They have medium to long ears and either a curly or straight tail. Their almond-shaped brown eyes are large and expressive.

Cockapoo coats can be many colors including black, white, apricot, chocolate, and cream. Some Cockapoo coats are solid color, while others have white and tan markings. The long, full hair is silky soft and slightly wavy.

Achoo!

Do dogs make you sneeze? No dog is completely **hypoallergenic**. But Cockapoos can be a good option for dog lovers with allergies. Most Cockapoos don't shed much, thanks to the low-shed coat of the Poodle. Because they shed less fur, they produce less dander. These skin flakes cause allergic reactions.

hypoallergenic—unlikely to cause allergic reactions

Chapter 4

Caring for a Cockapoo

Cockapoos are generally healthy dogs. But all dogs need yearly checkups with a veterinarian. The vet will give your dog **vaccinations** and check for health problems. Both Poodles and Cocker Spaniels can have knee and eye problems, so Cockapoos should be watched for these issues. Cockapoos are also prone to ear infections, like other dogs with long, floppy ears.

vaccination—a shot of medicine that protects animals from a disease

The veterinarian will also look at your Cockapoo's teeth. Dogs can't brush their own teeth, and they can develop dental problems. Some owners brush their dogs' teeth with toothpaste made for dogs. The vet will help you determine the best way to care for your dog's teeth.

BASIC NEEDS

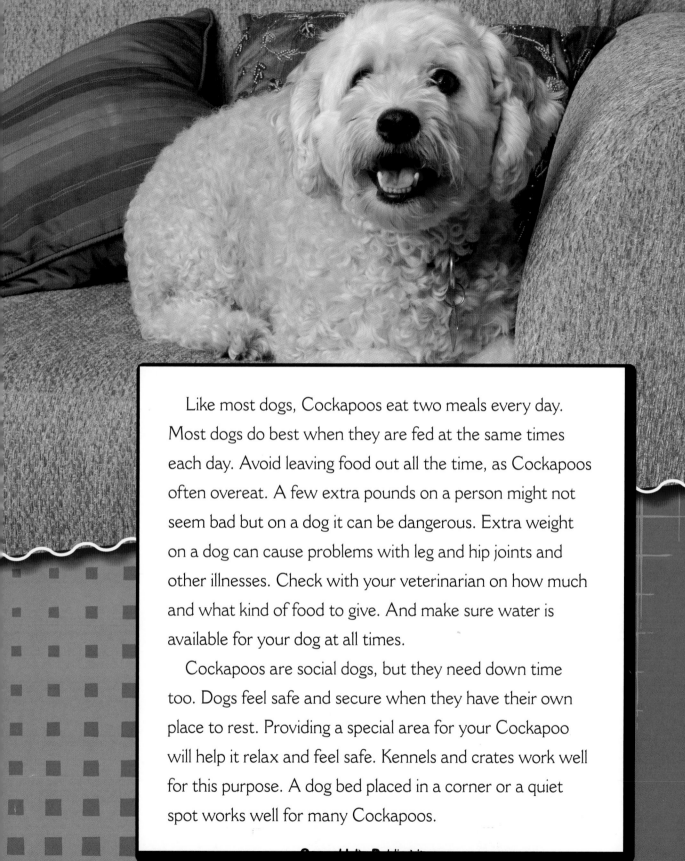

Like most dogs, Cockapoos eat two meals every day. Most dogs do best when they are fed at the same times each day. Avoid leaving food out all the time, as Cockapoos often overeat. A few extra pounds on a person might not seem bad but on a dog it can be dangerous. Extra weight on a dog can cause problems with leg and hip joints and other illnesses. Check with your veterinarian on how much and what kind of food to give. And make sure water is available for your dog at all times.

Cockapoos are social dogs, but they need down time too. Dogs feel safe and secure when they have their own place to rest. Providing a special area for your Cockapoo will help it relax and feel safe. Kennels and crates work well for this purpose. A dog bed placed in a corner or a quiet spot works well for many Cockapoos.

33 Hawthorne Avenue
Central Islip NY 11722

GET GROOMING

Cockapoos tend to have less odor than other dogs, but it is still important to keep them clean. They need a bath every two to three weeks. Bathing a dog too frequently can dry out its skin. Only shampoos made for dogs should be used to clean your Cockapoo.

After a bath is the best time to clip your Cockapoo's nails. Clippers made specifically for dogs work well for regular trimming. It's best to let an adult or professional groomer handle nail clipping. It can be difficult to keep the dog still and cut the nails properly. When nails are cut too short, they can bleed and be painful.

SPECIAL CONSIDERATIONS

Many owners and Cockapoos enjoy grooming as relaxing one-on-one time. Daily brushing is a good way to spend some quiet time with your pet. Cockapoos have beautiful, shiny fur, but it can be a mess if it isn't brushed. To keep their fur free of **mats**, Cockapoos should be brushed every day. Their coats also need to be trimmed occasionally, which is best handled by a professional groomer or adult.

Cockapoos need extra care for their eyes and ears. A groomer, veterinarian, or other adult should trim the long hair around the Cockapoo's eyes. Trimming the hair will keep it from irritating your dog's eyes. It will also help your dog see clearly. Long, floppy Cockapoo ears tend to get infections, so be sure to keep them clean and dry. A groomer can shave in and around the ear. A veterinarian can show you how to keep the ears clean.

mat—a thick, tangled mess of hair

EXERCISE

Cockapoos are smart and athletic dogs. They need physical and mental exercise to stay healthy and happy. A long daily walk can provide your Cockapoo with both. Walking is great exercise for a dog, but it also offers interesting sights, sounds, and smells. Dogs also have a strong **instinct** to walk with their **packs**. Pet dogs consider their human family their pack, so regular walks will strengthen your bond with your Cockapoo. Just be sure to use a collar and leash. Cockapoos like to follow scents and can get lost or injured if they take off without you.

Playtime is another good way to provide exercise for these athletic dogs. Cockapoos will play fetch and chase you until they can't run anymore. Some dogs enjoy swimming. The Cockapoo's Poodle parent is a natural in the water. Your Cockapoo might enjoy the water too.

instinct—behavior that is natural rather than learned
pack—a group of animals that lives and hunts together

In Training

The most loveable dog will never be a good housemate if not trained. Intelligence runs on both sides of the Cockapoo family, so these dogs are quick learners. A Cockapoo is eager to please and will train easily if you are patient and consistent. Because Cockapoos are sensitive, show encouraging emotions during training. Give positive rewards, such as dog treats, petting, and praise.

Chapter 5

A Member of the Family

Are you ready to welcome a dog into your family? If so, have a family discussion to decide what kind of dog will be the best fit. To be a responsible dog owner, do your homework. Research which breed will fit best in your family. Learn about the type of care different dogs need. Every dog is different, and the same is true for families. A little research will help to create a happy future for your family and your new pet.

If you want a Cockapoo, or if you're not quite sure, check out an animal shelter. Every year, millions of dogs become homeless. Purebreds, designer dogs, and mutts all end up in shelters and with rescue groups. You might find another mixed breed dog that you like. If so, read up on the parent breeds. A mutt might not be a mix of purebreds, but you can still get an idea of what the dog will be like.

Should You Adopt a Cockapoo?

Answer the questions below honestly. The more "yes" answers you have, the more likely a Cockapoo is the right dog for you.

1. Do you have time to cuddle and brush a dog every day?
2. Is your home a safe place for a sensitive and smart dog?
3. Are you willing to play with and walk a dog each day?
4. Do you want a dog that doesn't shed much?
5. Do you have the patience to train a dog?
6. Are you willing to commit to taking care of a dog for 14 to 18 years?

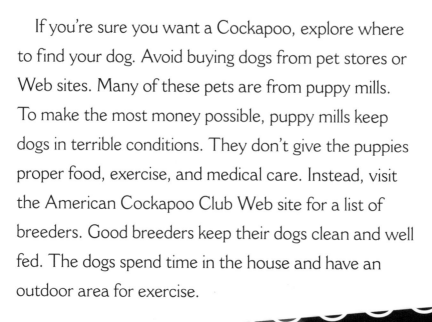

If you're sure you want a Cockapoo, explore where to find your dog. Avoid buying dogs from pet stores or Web sites. Many of these pets are from puppy mills. To make the most money possible, puppy mills keep dogs in terrible conditions. They don't give the puppies proper food, exercise, and medical care. Instead, visit the American Cockapoo Club Web site for a list of breeders. Good breeders keep their dogs clean and well fed. The dogs spend time in the house and have an outdoor area for exercise.

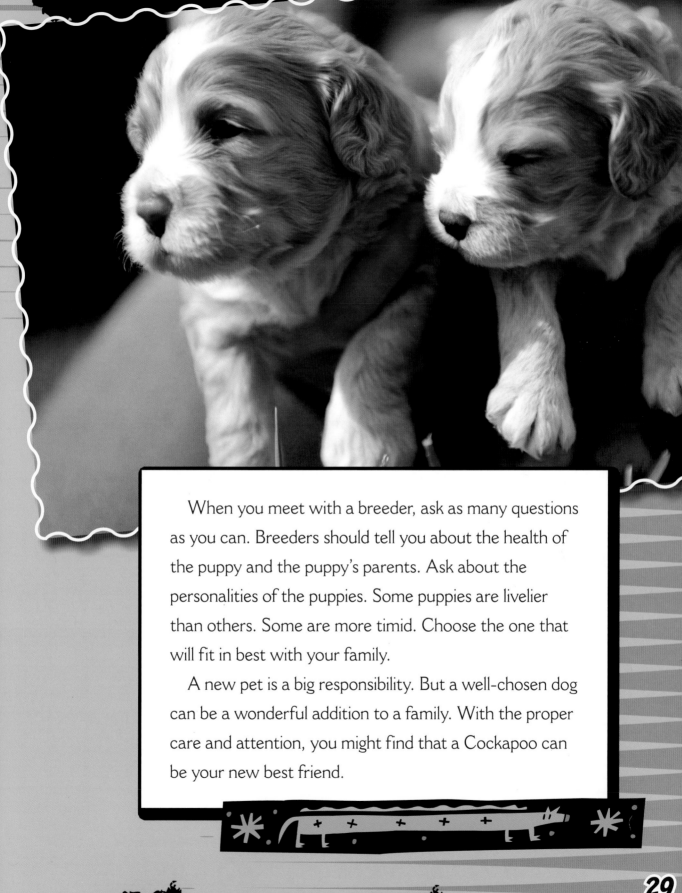

When you meet with a breeder, ask as many questions as you can. Breeders should tell you about the health of the puppy and the puppy's parents. Ask about the personalities of the puppies. Some puppies are livelier than others. Some are more timid. Choose the one that will fit in best with your family.

A new pet is a big responsibility. But a well-chosen dog can be a wonderful addition to a family. With the proper care and attention, you might find that a Cockapoo can be your new best friend.

Glossary

breed (BREED)—a certain kind of animal within an animal group; breed also means to mate and raise a certain kind of animal

hypoallergenic (hye-poh-a-luhr-JEN-ik)—unlikely to cause allergic reactions

instinct (IN-stingkt)—behavior that is natural rather than learned

mat (MAT)—a thick, tangled mass of fur

pack (PAK)—a group of animals that lives and hunts together

purebred (PYOOR-bred)—having parents of the same breed

temperament (TEM-pur-uh-muhnt)—the combination of an animal's behavior and personality

therapy dog (THER-uh-pee DAWG)—a dog trained to provide affection and comfort to people in need

trait (TRATE)—a quality or characteristic that makes one person or animal different from another

vaccination (vak-suh-NAY-shun)—a shot of medicine that protects animals from a disease

Read More

Landau, Elaine. *Poodles Are the Best!* The Best Dogs Ever. Minneapolis: Lerner, 2010.

Stone, Lynn. *Cocker Spaniels.* Eye to Eye with Dogs. Vero Beach, Fla.: Rourke Pub., 2009.

Wheeler, Jill. *Cockapoos.* Dogs. Edina, Minn.: ABDO Pub., 2008.

Internet Sites

FactHound offers a safe, fun way to find Internet sites related to this book. All of the sites on FactHound have been researched by our staff.

Here's all you do:

Visit *www.facthound.com*

Type in this code: 9781429677639

Super-cool stuff! Check out projects, games and lots more at **www.capstonekids.com**

Index